RAMADAN
COOKBOOK

THIS BOOK BELONGS TO

_____

_____

_____

TABLE OF CONTENTS

Bohra Fried Chicken, soft and succulent

Keema Naan

Chicken Penne Pasta Recipe with white sauce

Spinach Chicken Lasagne Recipe

Savory Chicken Crepe Recipe

Tikka Paratha roll bake recipe

Bread Lasagna with chicken and veggies

Lagan Ki Seekh

Lagan ki seekh (gluten free)

Dabba Chicken Pie

Bohra Red Chicken

Cheesy Spaghetti Balls Recipe

Maggie Noodle Omelet

Batata Vada (The BEST)

Prep: 20 minutes

Cook: 20 minutes

Total Time: 40 minutes

Servings: balls

Ingredients

- Four medium-sized potatoes (500 g), peeled and cooked.

Tempering

- 1 tbsp oil for frying
- Two curry leaf twigs or 2 tbsp cilantro
- 1/2 teaspoons of mustard seeds, if desired
- If desired, one teaspoon fennel seeds
- Two green chilies, finely chopped
- 1/2 tsp. garlic paste
- 1/2 teaspoon crushed red pepper
- 1/2 teaspoon cumin powder
- 1/2 teaspoon coriander powder
- One teaspoon turmeric powder
- 1 1/2 teaspoon salt

Other

- One medium peeled and coarsely chopped onion
- One teaspoon sugar
- Two tablespoons lemon juice

Coating

- One tablespoon gram flour

- 1/2 tsp salt.
- 1/2 tsp. red chili
- 1/2 teaspoon cumin
- If desired, add 1/2 teaspoon baking soda for crispness.
- Observe the notes.
- 1/2 cup water (or as needed)

Instructions

1. Using a potato masher, mash the boiling potatoes until smooth and set aside.

For tempting

1. In a saucepan, heat the oil and add garlic and mustard. Shortly after, add the other tempering ingredients.1 minute of vigorous stirring

2. Stir in the chopped onions until well combined, then remove from heat.

3. To temper, add the mashed potatoes, sugar, and lemon juice. Combine them and roll them into 15 tiny balls. Freeze for 10 minutes before using.

Make coating batter

1. Meanwhile, prepare the coating batter by whisking together all of the coating ingredients in a bowl. Make a drop-like batter.

Fry Batata Vada

1. In a nonstick wok or saucepan, heat about 2 inches of oil. Dip each potato ball in chickpea flour batter. With a wooden spatula, carefully lift it. Slowly lower the ball into the heated oil, careful not to damage it.

2. In batches, fry 4-5 balls at a time. Oil should be spooned over the ball but not stirred until solid. Then turn the ball over and heat it until golden on both sides.

3. Remove from the oil and pat dry. Immediately serve with chutney or condiment of choice.

Gobi Manchurian

Prep: 15 minutes

Cook: 30 minutes

Total Time: 45 minutes

Ingredients

For fried cauliflower

- 600g cauliflower florets; 1 medium cauliflower weighing 750 g yields approximately 600 g when chopped into florets.
- 6 tbsp. flour
- Six tablespoons cornstarch or rice flour
- 3/4 tsp Kashmiri chili, primarily for color; paprika can be substituted.
- 1 tsp red chili powder
- One teaspoon minced ginger
- One teaspoon minced garlic
- 1 tsp. salt
- frying oil

For gravy

- Two tablespoons oil
- One tablespoon minced garlic
- 1/3 tablespoons cumin seeds
- 1/2 cup finely diced onion
- 1/2 cups of finely sliced capsicum or bell peppers
- Two tablespoons finely chopped green chilies

Seasonings for sauces and gravies

- Two tablespoons ketchup
- Two tablespoons chili and garlic sauce
- 2–3 tablespoons mild chili sauce
- Three tablespoons soy sauce
- Two tablespoons vinegar
- 1/2 tablespoons sugar
- Pepper, to tasting
- Season with salt to taste.
- 2 tsp. cornflour
- 4 tsp water as needed to thin the gravy.
- 1/2 cup chopped green onions

Instructions

Cauliflower Blanching

1. Add the cauliflower florets and salt to boiling water. Allow boiling for about 2-3 minutes before transferring the florets to a kitchen towel to dry.

For cauliflower fried

1. combine ordinary flour, maize flour, Kashmiri chilies, red chilies, garlic, and ginger in a mixing bowl.

2. Set aside three tablespoons of the dry mix's flour mixture. Gradually add a little water to the dry ingredients and whisk thoroughly. Create a thick, flowing mixture.

4. Gently fold the blanched florets into the batter.

5. Sift the divided flour into the batter and stir to combine.

6. In a wok, heat oil over medium-high heat. Then add cauliflower florets one by one. On medium heat, fry cauliflower for two minutes.

7. Then transfer to a kitchen towel to cool. (At this point, the cauliflower should be a light golden color.)

Prepare gravy.

1. In a saucepan, heat two tablespoons of oil and add garlic and cumin. Sauté garlic for 30-60 seconds, or until golden.

2. Add the onions, bell peppers, and green chilies and cook for another 1-2 minutes.

3. Finally, combine all of the saucer section's components.

For use with slurry:

1. In a bowl, combine maize and water to form a slurry free of lumps. Contribute to the gravy. Additionally, add 1/4 cup of water as needed to get the appropriate consistency.

2. Boil the gravy for 2-3 minutes before removing it from the heat and reserving it.

Assemble

1. Just before serving, reheat the gravy and set it aside. Simultaneously, heat the oil in the wok to a very high temperature. Cooked cauliflower for 30 seconds more. Work in bunches of 2-3.

3. Transfer cauliflower flour to a kitchen towel after removing it from the oil. Then add the heated gravy. Coat thoroughly and garnish with chopped green onions. Serve it right away.

Fried Potatoes Recipe, Arabic style

Prep: 7 minutes

Cook: 15 minutes

Total Time: 22 minutes

Ingredients

- 1/2 kg potato, peeled and cubed
- 1/2 tsp salt.
- Cooking oil

Seasoning

- 1 tsp roasted and crushed cumin
- 1/2 teaspoons crushed coriander
- 1/2 tbsp. crushed red pepper
- 1/4 teaspoon salt
- 2–3 tablespoons chopped fresh coriander
- Lemons, freshly squeezed

Instructions

1. Wash, peel, and cube potatoes.

2. In a wok, heat oil with salt. Fry potato pieces for 2-3 minutes on a medium heat setting. Then continue frying for 2-3 minutes on high heat, or until brown on both sides. (Alternatively, poke it with a fork to determine tenderness.) Two batches of work are required.

3. In a small saucepan, dry roast cumin, coriander, red chili flakes, and salt for a few seconds.

4. Stir in fried potatoes and fresh coriander leaves. Season generously.

5. Serve immediately, garnished with lemon wedges.

Potato cheese balls recipe

Prep: 40 minutes

Cook: 5 minutes

Total Time: 45 minutes

Servings: balls (6 servings)

Ingredients

- 500 grams potatoes

Seasoning:

- 3-4 tablespoons bread crumbs
- 2 tbsp. chopped fresh coriander
- Two tablespoons finely sliced green onions
- Two tablespoons lemon juice
- 1/2 tbsp of red chili powder
- One teaspoon minced garlic
- One teaspoon cumin powder
- 3/4 teaspoon salt

Regarding cheese

- 100 g cheddar cheese, cubed
- 1/4 teaspoon crushed red pepper
- 1/4 teaspoon dried basil
- 1/4 tsp freshly ground black pepper

To cover

- 2 tbsp of cornflour
- 1-2 eggs, as needed
- 1/4 teaspoon red chili powder
- 1/4 teaspoon salt
- One tablespoons water
- 1 pound breadcrumbs
- Cooking oil

Instructions

1. In a big saucepan, wash and boil the potatoes with salt. Peel and mash potatoes until smooth. (For further information, see the suggestions above the recipe card.)

2. Combine all spice ingredients in a meshed potato and thoroughly mix.

For Cheese

Cut the cheese into twenty pieces. Season cheese by using red chili, black pepper, and herbs.

Potato Rolls with Potato Balls

2. Using mashed potatoes, roll 20 balls while simultaneously putting cheese cubes into each ball. Assemble the cheese cube so that it is entirely coated with potato.

3. two-layer bread crumb coating

4. In a mixing bowl, combine eggs, salt, red chili powder, and water. Place aside.

5. First, coat all of the balls in cornflour. Coat each ball in egg wash, then bread crumbs.

6. To coat each ball twice, dip it first in egg wash and then in bread crumbs.

7. Refrigerate the balls for 30 minutes to harden them up.

To fry

a.   Two minutes on medium heat, then 1 minute on high heat, or until golden and crisp.

To Freeze

1. Place the unfired balls on a tray and place them in the freezer for 2 hours. Now seal the balls in a container or a zip-lock bag. These balls may be stored in the freezer for up to a month. Fry frozen balls straight

on medium heat without thawing. Frozen balls will require more time to cook.

Lamb or Beef Keema Samosa Recipe

Prep: 20 minutes

Cook: 15 minutes

Total Time: 35 minutes

Servings: or 14 Samosa

Ingredients

For Qeema filling

- 250 g minced lamb or beef
- a quarter cup of water

Spices

- 1 tbsp. fresh ginger garlic paste
- 1/2 tablespoons of roasted and ground coriander
- 1/2 tbsp cumin, roasted and ground
- 1/2 teaspoon red chili powder
- 1/2 tsp. Garam Masala
- 1/4 teaspoon turmeric
- 3/4 teaspoon salt to taste

Other

- 1 cup onion, finely chopped
- a third of a cup coarsely chopped green onion
- 1/4 cup chopped green coriander
- 2 tbsp. chopped mint leaves
- One teaspoon chat masala (or to taste)

- One teaspoon lemon juice
- 2-3 tablespoons of coarsely chopped green chilies
- samosa patties or spring roll wraps (approximately 12 to 14)
- 2 tbsp wheat flour, combined with a small amount of water to form a paste. cooking oil

Instructions

1. In a saucepan, combine mince, water, and the ingredients listed under the spices list. Cook for 15 to 20 minutes over medium heat or until the water evaporates. Take the pan off the heat.

2. Immediately combine the remaining ingredients for the somas to fill the heated mince.

3. Insist on filling and folding. Seal with a wheat flour/water paste.

4. Fry samosas in small batches for 3 minutes over medium heat or crispy.

5. Transfer them to a paper towel to absorb any remaining oil. Serve immediately.

Reminders to store:

1. Uncooked samosas can be refrigerated for up to 24 hours.

2. Alternatively, frozen for two months. Separately freeze them on a tray and then transfer them to a freezer bag.

3. Fried samosas may be kept on the counter for 6–8 hours in a paper bag. Reheat in the oven or re-fry in the deep fryer.

Samosas To bake:

Preheat the oven to 350°F.Spray both sides of the samosa with oil. After that, arrange the samosas on a baking sheet coated with butter paper. heated oven for 15-20 minutes until crispy and golden. After 10 minutes, flip the samosa to ensure even cooking.

Fried Eggplant Fries Recipe

Prep: 15 minutes

Cook: 10 minutes

Total Time: 25 minutes

Ingredients

- 2 (200 gram) eggplant

Soaking solution

- Two tablespoons water
- 1/2 cup milk
- 1/4 teaspoon salt

Flour Coating

- 1/2 cup all-purpose flour
- One chicken cube or bulge, or one tablespoon of chicken powder
- 1/2 teaspoon dried basil leaves

Bread crumbs as a coating

- 1-2 eggs
- One tablespoon milk
- 3. a pinch of salt
- 1 pound breadcrumbs
- Oil for frying

Accompaniment

- Masala Chaat
- Ketchup

Instructions

1. In a big bowl, mix milk, water, and salt.

2. Peel and cut the eggplant lengthwise like you would cut french fries. For 10 minutes, soak the eggplant in a milk water solution.

3. In a mixing bowl, combine all flour coating ingredients. Wipe the eggplant slices dry with a paper towel and cover each piece with a flour coating. Combine eggs, salt, pepper, and milk in a mixing bowl. Coat each eggplant slice first with the egg mixture and the bread crumbs.

5. Once all the fries are covered, heat the oil in a deep fryer and deep fry the eggplant fries until golden brown. Serve with ketchup and chat masala on the side.

Chapli Kabab Recipe

Prep: 15 minutes

Cook: 15 minutes

Resting time: 30 minutes

Total Time: 1 hour

Ingredients

Whole Spices

- 1 1/2 tbsp dried pomegranate arils (anar dana), which can be used in place of dry mango powder
- To taste, 1 1/2 to 2 tbsp red chili flakes
- One tablespoon cumin seeds
- One tablespoon coriander seeds
- 1/2 tbsp. fennel seeds (Sauf)

Spices ground

- For 1/2 tbsp of Kashmiri chili powder (for color, substitute with paprika)

- One teaspoon red chili powder (omit if you prefer a milder flavor).
- One teaspoon garam masala
- One teaspoon black, pink
- 1 tsp freshly ground black pepper
- 1/2 tsp. turmeric powder

Regarding Kabab

- 1/2 kilogram minced meat (lamb or beef)20%-30% fat
- 1 cup chopped onion, about one large, wring out any excess moisture (if any), and discard
- 1 cup maize meal (makai ka atta)
- 2 tbsp ginger-garlic paste
- 2 tbsp. chopped fresh coriander
- Six tablespoons finely chopped green chili
- 2 tbsp. butter (or clarified butter)
- 3/4 cup chopped tomato (approximately one tomato)
- Ghee or butter for frying, authentically fried in tallow

Instructions

For spice mix

1. Toast cumin, coriander, pomegranate aril, and fennel seeds for 1 minute in a small saucepan. Take the pan off the heat.

2. Immediately add the ground spices to the heated pan and swirl for a few seconds. Transfer spices to a food processor and pulse briefly until a coarse powder forms. Place aside.

For Chapli kabab

1. Combine mince, spice mixture, green chilies, ginger, garlic, onions, fresh coriander, and butter in a large mixing bowl. Allow 30 minutes for marinating. (Ideally, 4-6 hours.)

2. Before cooking, add the tomato, egg, and cornmeal. Combine well until the mince reaches a dough-like consistency.

3. Pro tip: Deep-fry a small amount of kabab and taste it. Adjust as necessary. This is an optional step.

4. Roll out kabab balls and flatten them with your palms.

5. On a medium burner, shallow fry kababs in clarified butter or fat for 2-3 minutes, or until crispy and lightly browned.

Notes

stor chapli kabab

Cooked Chapli kabab should be refrigerated in an airtight container. Reheat in a covered dish in the microwave before serving. Additionally, you may freeze it for up to two months.

Shami Kebab Recipe

Prep: 20 minutes

Cook: 45 minutes

Rolling and Frying: 20 minutes

Total Time: 1 hour 25 minutes

Ingredients

Shami kebab Spice Mix Recipe

- One teaspoon red chili powder or 6–8 red round chilies
- Five cloves languid
- a broken two-inch cinnamon stick

- One large black cardamom
- 1/2 teaspoon black pepper, freshly ground
- a single bay leaf (optional)
- One tablespoon coriander seeds
- One teaspoon cumin
- One teaspoon cumin
- If desired, sprinkle with 1/2 teaspoon fenugreek seeds or
- One teaspoon salt

Meat Cooking

- 500 g of boneless beef, cubed, preferably chuck roast or lamb shank
- 250 g yellow split peas (1 1/4 cups) soaked in warm water for 2 hours
- One potato, peeled and chunked
- 4 tbsp Shami Kebab Spice Mix, to taste
- 2 tbsp olive oil
- 1/2 tbsp. of mint leaves
- Three green chilies (or one tablespoon green chili paste)
- Ginger root 2 inch or ginger paste (1/2 teaspoon)
- Four garlic cloves, preferably fat, or 1 tsp garlic paste
- 1/2 teaspoon turmeric
- 1 cup of water

Creating kabab

- Three tablespoons of freshly chopped coriander
- One teaspoon chat masala, or to taste
- One diced onion (approximately 1 cup)
- One beaten egg
- 1hard-boiled eggs, sliced

Fry kebabs

- Three eggs (for the egg wash).
- 1/4 teaspoon salt
- 1/4 teaspoon chili powder
- Optional breadcrumbs
- Cooking oil

Instructions

The Recipe for Spice Mix

1. On medium heat, toast the whole spices for 1-2 minutes or until aromatic. Then grind the roasted spice with a coffee grinder. The masala, or spice blend, for Shami Kebab, is prepared.

Meat preparation

1. Combine all beef-cooking ingredients in a big saucepan. To cook the meat and yellow split peas for 45 minutes,

With continual stirring, burn out any extra water. This is a critical stage.

2. Allow the kebab mixture to cool for a few minutes. Then, using a chopper, puree the yellow split peas and beef.

Creating kebabs

1. Toss the kebab mixture with the mint, fresh coriander, hard-boiled egg, one beaten egg, and salt. Combine thoroughly.

2. Grease your hands with oil and shape the mixture into kebabs.

3. Deep-fry kebabs

4. In a mixing bowl, combine eggs, salt, and red chili powder.

5. Coat each kebab with an egg, then bread crumbs. (If bread crumbs are used.)

6. Fry each kebab until golden brown in a small amount of oil and serve immediately.

Notes

1. Spices including fenugreek, cumin, and cardamon should be avoided. You may also use red chili flakes or powder in place of the red button chile. Ridge.

Meat:

1. Use tough stewing meat like a piece of beef, a roast of meat, or a beef shank. Additionally, boneless mutton or chicken breast is available. If you choose lean meat, you must add oil when making the kebabs, or else the kababs will be too dry.

2. You may substitute ground beef (keema), but the thread will be lost (resha). If using ground beef, mash the ingredients with a potato masher until smooth. Drying extra water from ground beef is critical while forming kebabs.

3. The primary component in shami kebab is yellow split pea. It is also known as channa dal and is not confused with chickpeas.

4. Freeze the kebabs in a single layer in a dish.

5. Once the kebabs are entirely frozen, place them in a zipper bag and freeze them for two months.

6. Thaw frozen kababs for 15 minutes on the counter before frying. On low heat, deep fry Shami kabab until brown and well cooked. If you fry kabab on high heat, the exterior will be golden, and the interior will be chilly. Therefore, avoid this. One visual indicator that frozen kababs have been wholly cooked is that the middle coating should be golden, just like the outside, and not seem raw.

Keema cutlet, soft and juicy

Prep: 30 minutes

Cook: 10 minutes

Total Time: 40 minutes

Servings: cutlets

Ingredients

- 1/2 kg (1.1 pounds) of mutton, beef, or lamb mincemeat (keema).
- 4-5 bread slices (preferably Karak roti)
- 1/2 c. milk

Spices

- One tablespoon Hari Mirch (green chili paste)
- One tablespoon ginger-garlic paste
- 1/2 tsp coriander powder (dhania)
- 1/2 tbsp red pepper, or to taste (Kuti Lal Mirch)
- One teaspoon cumin powder
- 1/2 tsp. black pepper (kali Mirch)
- 1/2 teaspoon turmeric powder (Haldi)
- 1/2–1 teaspoon red chili powder (Lal Mirch)
- 1/2 tsp salt (or to taste)

Herbs

- 2 tbsp fresh green coriander (hara dhania)
- 2 tsp fresh mint (pudina) leaves

Other

- 4 tbsp freshly squeezed lemon juice
- One egg, for incorporation into mince marination
- 1 cup bread crumbs (for rolling the cutlets)

For frying

- Three large eggs, separated into white and yolk for the egg wash
- 1/4 teaspoon salt
- 1/4 teaspoon red chili powder (or pepper)
- Cooking oil

Instructions

Preparing the mixture for the cutlets

1. Soak bread in milk and mash it; set aside.

2. In a food processor, pulse the beef mince and spices until the mince is very fine and mushy.

3. Add soaked bread, cilantro, mint, lemon juice, and one egg to ground mince. Mix mince and spices thoroughly with your hands. The mixture should be soft, similar to roti dough.

4. Cook a cutlet ball to test the salt and spice levels. If necessary, adjust the mixture to taste at this point. This is an optional step.

Shaping Cutlets

1. On a dish, spread bread crumbs. Then, using a tiny amount of the mince mixture, form a small ball. Cover this ball with bread crumbs and place it on the bread crumb platter. Press the ball into a round, thin disc approximately 3 inches in diameter with your fingers. Likewise, prepare all of the cutlets.

Frying cutlets

1. Heat the oil in a saucepan.
2. Hand-beat the egg whites until foamy. Combine the egg yolk, salt, and pepper generously.
3. Brush each cutlet with egg and shallow fry for 4 minutes on each side over medium heat. Then drain and serve it on a paper towel.

Notes

1. The cutlet can be stored in the freezer for up to 2 months.

2. After drying the oil, wrap the cutlets in foil and serve them. You may reheat the cutlets by steaming them on the stovetop. This method ensures that the cutlets remain moist and tender.

3. Because oil tends to bubble up while frying cutlets, separating the yolk and white of an egg helps address this issue.

Chicken Seekh Kabab Recipe Pan-fried or Baked

Prep: 30 minutes

Cook: 30 minutes

Total Time: 1 hour

Servings: wooden skewer kabab

Equipment

- a chopstick, a pencil, or metal skewers

Ingredients

Ingredients for marination

- 500 g white chicken fat ground chicken
- One medium onion, coarsely chopped; squeeze out excess water and discard.
- 3 tbsp fresh coriander, finely chopped
- Two tablespoons minced ginger
- 2 tbsp. minced garlic (lahsun)
- 1-2 green chilies, finely chopped
- Three tablespoons butter
- Two tablespoons cream
- Three tablespoons seekh kabab masalaYou may also use ready-made.

- ghee or vegetable oil for frying
- 2-inch chunk of charcoal to smoke

Seekh kabab masala recipe

- 3 tbsp gram flour (besan) or chickpea flour
- One tablespoon coriander seeds
- Color: 1 tablespoon powdered Kashmiri red chilies or paprika
- 3/4 tbsp red chili powder, plus more to taste
- 1/2 tablespoons cumin seeds
- 1 tsp freshly ground black pepper
- 1/2 tsp. turmeric powder.
- 1/4 tsp oregano seed (ijma)
- Four cloves, long
- One teaspoon salt, or to taste

Masala Instructions

1. 1 minute, stirring frequently, roast all ingredients for seekh kabab masala. (Gram flour burns fast, so use caution.) Remove to a dish to cool before finely grinding in a spice grinder. The spice mixture for seekh kabab is prepared.

Marination

2. In a dish, place your ground chicken. Combine the ginger, onion, butter, cream, Seekh kabab masala, garlic, green chilies, and coriander in a medium mixing bowl.

3. Combine well—Cook a small amount of the mixture in a frying pan to test it. Salt and seekh kabab masala to taste. Then marinate the chicken mixture in the refrigerator for 20-30 minutes.

Method 1:

Seekh kabab recipe (stovetop or pan-fried)

1. Prepare charcoal for smoking by heating it over an open flame. If you are a smoker,

2. Oil your hand. Using a pencil, chopstick, or skewer, form a long, cylindrical kabab from the marinated mixture.

3. 2 tbsp oil in a medium saucepan. Fry seeks kabab until brown on all sides over medium-high heat.

4. Fry all the kababs in batches, wrap them in aluminum foil, and smoke them over charcoal.

In an oven, Method 2

1. Preheat oven to 300F. Cook roll kababs for 10 minutes, or until firm and brown. To ensure consistent cooking, flip the kabab halfway through. Serve immediately after smoking.

To Barbecue Seekh Kabab (Optional Step)

1. In a skillet or saucepan, combine all the kababs. In between the kababs, place the red-hot charcoal on the foil. Now immediately sprinkle a few drops of oil over 2. the coals and seal the pot. The smoke must remain contained within the bank.

3. After 5 minutes of smoking, remove the lid and serve with raita or chutney.

Notes

1. Ground chicken dripping with fat: To make juicy seekh kababs, chicken ground with white chicken fat is necessary. I used boneless chicken and crushed it with white fat around the bird in a food processor.

1. For this dish, we'll need finely chopped onions. I diced the onion in a food processor and pressed it lightly between my palms to remove extra moisture.

2. I also diced the ginger and garlic separately in a food processor. If the chopped ginger is watery, softly squeeze it to remove the liquid.

Cassoulet kabab instructions

1. These kababs may be prepared up to a day in advance. Transfer the kababs to a casserole dish and top with onion rings. Drizzle the kabab with a couple of teaspoons of tamarind chutney, garlic raita, or green chutney. Wrap the container in foil and refrigerate for 12–18 hours. Preheat the oven to 250 F just before serving. Place the kabab in the oven and bake for 15–20 minutes, or until hot. Serve with salads and raita.

Freezing instructions

Prep: 15 minutes

Cook: 30 minutes

Resting Time: 4 hours

Total Time: 45 minutes

Servings: serving (14)

Ingredients

For Marination

- 500 g minced ground beef, lamb, or mutton, 20% fat
- 2 tbsp. Butter or ghee.
- an individual egg
- Three tablespoons chickpea flour (besan)
- Three tablespoons grated ginger
- One tablespoon minced garlic
- 1/2 tsp. red chili powder
- 1/2 teaspoon cumin powder
- 1/2 teaspoon coriander powder

- One teaspoon turmeric powder
- Two tablespoons lemon juice
- One teaspoon salt

Other

- 1/2 cup finely chopped onion
- Four tablespoons chopped coriander leaves
- Two tablespoons minced mint

<u>Instructions</u>

1. Using a food processor, mince all marinade ingredients until fine and dough-like.

2. Mix the remaining ingredients.

3. Place this mixture in a basin. Refrigerate it for 4 hours or overnight.

4. Fry a tiny kabab patty and do a taste test. If necessary, adjust the salt or spices.

5. Roll the dough into balls.

6. Using a pencil or chopstick, mash each ball until it becomes a long, cylindrical kebab approximately 5 inches long.

7. Carefully take the kebab out of the pencil and place it on a platter.

Pan-fried (Recommended Method)

1. In a nonstick skillet, heat one tablespoon of oil and cook 4-5 kebabs in batches. Flip kebabs as needed to ensure even cooking until golden. Remove the kebab and serve with hot kebab right away.

Baked:

2. Preheat the oven to 350°F.

3. Arrange the kebabs in a baking dish or casserole. 4. Apply a thin coating of oil to the kebab. Baked kebabs on the middle shelf for 20 minutes. Half-roll kebabs to ensure consistent cooking.

4. To get a naturally grilled appearance, pan-sear the chicken until brown on both sides.

5. You may also broil kebabs on the top level of the oven, but I found that this method dries them out.

smoke (optional)

1. To smoke pan-fried or baked kebabs, heat a package of charcoal until one corner is red.

2. In a pot, gather kebab and add a piece of foil to the center. Transfer the heated coal onto the foil carefully using tongs. Drizzle a little oil over the embers and cover the saucepan tightly. Allow 5-7 minutes for the kebab to smoke before serving.

Notes

Seekh kebabs are traditionally grilled over a grill pit. The kebabs are wrapped over seekh, a type of metal skewer. Use the same seasoned mince to make kebabs.

Freezing

2. Completely cook the kebab and allow it to come to room temperature before freezing.

3. To use, place frozen kebabs in a casserole dish. Arrange onion rings on top of the kebab and sprinkle with chutney. Additionally, tomato and chile slices are served on the side. Using a piece of red hot charcoal, smoke the food. Additionally, cover the dish with aluminum foil. Bake the kebab casserole for 20 minutes longer or until the kebabs, are well heated.

Kebab casserole:

Similarly, you may cook the kebab casserole a day ahead of time and keep it in the refrigerator. Bake until completely warm just before serving.

Aloo Keema Patties/Cutlets recipe

Prep: 20 minutes

Cook: 30 minutes

Cooling Time: 20 minutes

Total Time: 50 minutes

Ingredients

For Qeema filling

- 1/2 kg mince, 20% fat (mutton or beef or lamb)
- Spices
- 2 1/2 tablespoons ginger-garlic paste
- 1 tbsp powdered coriander (preferably toasted)
- a third of a teaspoon cumin powder
- 1 tbsp crushed red pepper, to taste
- One teaspoon Garam Masala Powder fat
- 1/2 tsp. turmeric powder
- 1 1/2 teaspoon salt (to taste)

Other

- One onion, chopped
- 3–4 medium-sized chopped green peppers
- 2-4 hard-boiled eggs, peeled and cut into tiny pieces
- 3/4 cups of coarsely chopped green onion
- 1/4 cup chopped green coriander

- 1/4 cup chopped mint leaves
- One teaspoon chat masala (or to taste)

For potatoes

- 2 kg cooked and peeled potatoes
- 2 tbsp. butter
- 2 tsp powdered red chili
- 4. salt to taste.

For coating

- 4-6 eggs
- 1/2 teaspoon red chili powder
- salt to taste.
- 2 tbsp. water
- 4 cup bread crumbs
- Oil for deep frying

Instructions for stuffing mince

1. Boil mince, spices, and 1/2 cup water for 20 minutes over medium heat. When the mince is tender, dry any leftover moisture on a high burner while stirring.

2. combine boiled eggs, green onions, green chilies, green coriander, onions, and mint with the hot mince. Stuffing is prepared.

For potatoes

1. Mash potatoes until smooth, then stir in red chili powder, salt, and butter.

Creating Pattie

1. Shape the potatoes into tiny balls.

2. Then, squeeze each ball and fill with two teaspoons of chopped filling using your palm. Pull the mashed potato edges together to create Patti or cutlets. It produces all patties in the same manner.

Double layer of bread crumbs

2. In a large mixing bowl, whisk together the eggs, red chili powder, and salt. Additionally, whisk two tablespoons of water into a thin egg wash.

3. Begin by dipping each burger in egg wash and then coating it with bread crumbs. Coat each patty with eggs again and bread crumbs for the final coat.

4. Refrigerate patties for 30 minutes. (If storing for a few hours, wrap in plastic wrap and keep in an airtight container.)

Add 2-3 inches of oil to a wok. After sufficiently heating the oil, gently cook each burger. 3–4 patties should be dipped in oil and allowed to firm up. For 1 minute, do not stir. Then, using a flat spatula, carefully turn the pan to cook the opposite side when all sides of the burger are crisp and brown. Transfer them to a kitchen towel and serve immediately.

Aloo Tikki Recipe

Prep: 10 minutes

Cook: 15 minutes

Chilling Time: 10 minutes

Total Time: 35 minutes

Ingredients

- four peeled and medium-cooked potatoes (500 g)

Tempering

- One tablespoon oil
- One medium peeled and coarsely chopped onion

- Two green chilies, finely chopped
- One tablespoon ginger-garlic paste
- 1/2 tbsp crushed red pepper
- 1/2 tsp. cumin powder
- 1/2 teaspoon coriander powder
- 1/2 tsp. turmeric powder
- 1 1/2 teaspoon salt

Other

- Four tablespoons bread crumbs
- 2 tsp cornstarch
- One tablespoon lemon juice
- 2 tbsp. chopped fresh coriander
- 1/2 tsp. Chat masala, or according to taste.

Instructions

1. Mash boiling potatoes with a potato masher until smooth. Place aside.

2. In a saucepan, heat the oil and add the tempering ingredients. Stir well and simmer for 1 minute. Take the pan off the heat.

3. Combine the mashed potatoes, tempering, and remaining ingredients in a mixing bowl. Combine them and roll out ten little tikkis. Refrigerate the mixture for 10 minutes to cool.

4. In small batches, fry the Tikki till brown and crispy. (Turn the Tikki after 1 minute in hot oil.) Drain on a towel and serve with your favorite sauce or chutney.

Notes

Additional variants:

Protein sources:

1. Alternatively, you may add a few teaspoons of leftover shredded chicken, mince, or shredded beef to the Tikki mixture.

Vegetarian options

1. Similarly, a few tablespoons of green peas or green onions can be added.

Ground chicken nugget (fried)

Prep: 30 minutes

Cook: 8 minutes

Total Time: 38 minutes

Servings: pieces

Ingredients

- 750 g boneless chicken breast (approximately three breasts) or 750 g ground chicken
- 3 tbsp finely sliced onion, liquid squeezed out and discarded, or 1/2 tsp onion powder
- 1 tsp garlic powder or 2 tsp garlic paste
- 1 1/2 teaspoons chicken powder or 1/2 cup chicken cubes/bullion with a small amount of cornflour
- Three tablespoons lemon juice
- 3/4 teaspoon salt (additional salt to taste)
- 1/2 tsp of pepper
- 2–3 large eggs for egg wash
- 3 cups bread crumbs (for coating)

Instructions

Chicken Meat

1. Pat dry the chicken breasts. Each breast should be cut into tiny pieces. Then, grind the mixture to a fine paste using a food processor. If using finely ground chicken, omit this step.

Salt and pepper the chicken on the ground.

2. In a large mixing bowl, combine the garlic, onions, lemon juice, salt, and pepper with the chicken mince. It's normal for the chicken mixture to be sticky. Place aside.

Prepare Breading Station

3. Whisk eggs in a dish with salt and pepper to make an egg wash. On a big platter, spread some bread crumbs. Keep a baking sheet or big tray on hand to place the prepared nuggets.

Roll out nuggets

4. Grease your hands with oil and form little balls from the crushed chicken mixture. Bread crumbs coat each ball. This will result in balls that are stiff enough to handle.

5. Using your hands, form the balls into squares or circles. Each nugget should be dipped in egg wash and then in bread crumbs.

Instructions for Frying

1. To fry, immediately drop a few nuggets into the heated oil. Avoid overcrowding the pot and cook for 2-3 minutes on medium heat. Heat to high and cook for 2 minutes more, or until golden. Avoid overcooking since this may result in dry nuggets.

2. Drain on a kitchen towel and serve with your favorite dip or ketchup right away.

Instructions for Freezing

1. Place the nuggets on a baking sheet and place them in the freezer for two hours or until rock solid. Avoid stacking the nuggets; keep them separate.

2. Freeze in plastic zip-lock bags or a container lined with layers of butter paper once frozen. Fry frozen nuggets straight in heated oil. on medium heat 4 min 2 minutes more on high heat, or until golden brown.

Hariyali Chicken Tikka Recipe

Prep: 10 minutes

Cook: 10 minutes

Resting Time: 20 minutes

Total Time: 40 minutes

Servings: skewers

Equipment

Wooden Skewers

Ingredients

- Two cubed chicken breasts (500 g)
- marinade paste in green
- 1 cup loosely packed cilantro leaves
- 1/2 cups of mint leaves, packed loosely
- To taste, 2–5 tiny fresh chilies or 1 1/2 tbsp green chili paste
- 4-5 garlic cloves, or 1/2 tablespoon of garlic paste
- 1/2 tbsp ginger paste or 1-inch ginger root
- One teaspoon toasted cumin seeds
- 3/4 teaspoon garam masala powder
- Two tablespoons lemon juice
- One teaspoon salt, or to taste

- 2 tbsp of cream or low-fat yogurt
- 2 tbsp oil, plus more for brushing when cooking.
- Water for grinding

Instructions

1. Rinse and dry the chicken.

2. Blend all items (excluding chicken) until smooth.

3. Drizzle the green marinade over the chicken and set aside for at least 20 minutes on the counter (or 4–12 hours in the fridge).

4. Skewer the chicken marinated in the marinade onto wooden skewers. (optional)

To cook in a skillet

1. Preheat a piece of charcoal to a red-hot temperature. (If you are a smoker)

2. On high heat for 8–10 minutes, turn the chicken after 4 minutes. When you notice scorched lines on the chicken, it is ready.

3. Use hot skewers to smoke the chicken in a saucepan. In the saucepan, arrange the red charcoal on top of a piece of foil. Drizzle a little oil over the heated coals and cover the saucepan. Allow the chicken to rest for 4-5 minutes before serving with any garlic dip of your choice.

4. To bake in the oven, heat the oven to 350 degrees F. Bake the chicken for 15-20 minutes, or until the water runs clear. To ensure equal cooking, flip the chicken halfway through. After baking, the chicken may be smoked.

To cook over a charcoal grill,

1. (Be careful to soak your wooden skewers in water for 4-6 hours to ensure they do not catch fire.)

2. Grill for 8 minutes or until browned.

Chicken Malai Tikka Boti

Prep: 45 minutes

Cook: 16 minutes

Total Time: 1 hour 1 minute

Servings: Skewers

Equipment

Eight wooden skewers

Ingredients

- 500-gram boneless chicken marinade
- 1 tbsp papaya paste or 1 tsp beef tenderizer
- 1 1/2–2 tbsp green chili paste, depending on heat preference
- One tablespoon ginger-garlic paste
- 1/2 tsp. cumin powder
- 1/2 teaspoon coriander powder
- 1/2 tsp freshly ground black pepper
- 1/2 tsp. garam masala
- One teaspoon cornstarch
- 1/2 chicken cubes or bouillon, if desired.
- 3/4 teaspoon salt, plus additional salt if using chicken cubes.
- 1/4 cup tablespoon greek yogurt or hanging curd
- 1/4 cup heavy cream
- Three tablespoons coarsely chopped onions, onion paste, or 1/2 teaspoon onion powder
- 1 tbsp chopped cilantro or fresh coriander

- 1 tbsp cream cheese, 1 tbsp cheese triangle, or 2 tbsp milk powder, to taste
- Two tablespoons lemon juice

Other

frying oil

Instructions

1. Rinse and pat dry the chicken cubes. (If using chicken breast, thoroughly wash and towel dry the chicken before cutting into 1-inch pieces.)

2. Combine all marinade ingredients.

3. Add the chicken and thoroughly combine; preferably marinate for 45 minutes to 2 hours. You may marinate the chicken up to 12 hours in advance and keep it in the refrigerator.

4. Skewer the chicken breasts onto the wooden skewers. Place aside.

5. In a nonstick skillet, heat the oil and add the tikka skewer. Cook the skewers for 3–4 minutes on medium heat, covered. Then, remove the lid and cook for 1-2 minutes on high heat, or until the water evaporates and the tikkas are gently brown. Prepared in batches

6. Serve immediately or smoke for 2 minutes over red hot charcoal with a sprinkle of oil.

Notes

1. Barbecue Grill: Malai tikka can be threaded onto metal skewers or wooden skewers. Simply soak a wooden skewer in water for 4-6 hours. Then arrange Malai both skewers in a grilling basket or cage. Grill the chicken for 5-7 minutes, until cooked through and charred. Continue turning to ensure even cooking.

2. Bake skewered malai tikka for 15 minutes on a preheated 350°F oven center rack. After 8 minutes, flip the tikka halfway through for even cooking.

3. The marinated chicken can be made into a malai tikka curry by adding more spices, yogurt, cream, or coconut milk. Similarly, you may prepare a gravy version of leftover fried malai tikka.

4. The Malai Tikka is frequently served at significant events, and the recipe doubles or triples easily.

Dynamite Chicken Recipe

Prep: 15 minutes

Cook: 10 minutes

Total Time: 25 minutes

Ingredients

- 500 g cubed boneless skinless chicken breast
- 1/2 tsp baking powder
- Sauce dynamite
- 3/4 cup mayonnaise
- 4 tbsp Sriracha sauce (or more to taste)
- Two tablespoons ketchup
- 1/2 tbsp of honey
- Garlic powder or paste 1/2 tsp

Marination

- One tablespoon soy sauce
- One tablespoon paprika
- One teaspoon garlic powder

- One teaspoon salt
- 1/2 tsp dried herbs used oregano.

Flour Coating

- 1/2 cups of whole wheat flour
- 1/2 cups cornstarch/cornflour
- 1/2 teaspoon black pepper, freshly ground
- 1/2 teaspoon salt

Using an egg wash

- Two eggs,
- 1/4 teaspoon salt
- 1/2 teaspoons dried herbs
- 1/4 teaspoon salt;
- Oil for frying
- 4-5 tablespoons fresh lettuce
- Green onion (as a garnish)

Instructions

Velvet ting: (optional)

Combine baking powder and chicken in a bowl. Allow 20 minutes. Then thoroughly wash the chicken under running tap water. In a colander, strain the chicken's water. Set it aside and pat it dry with a kitchen towel.

Create an awe-inspiring sauce:

1. Set aside the dynamite sauce ingredients in a basin.
2. Mari nation: In a bowl, combine the marinade ingredients and chicken. Combine thoroughly and set aside until needed.

Flour Coating:

1. On a plate, combine all of the flour coating ingredients. Place aside.

2. Set aside the egg wash ingredients after beating the eggs.

Assemble

1. Egg wash the marinated chicken first. Then wholly coat it with the flour mixture.

2. Fry chicken until crispy in heated oil over medium-high heat. Transfer the chicken to a serving platter. Serve with a drizzle of sauce.

3. Alternatively, you may cover the chicken thoroughly in sauce. In an ice cream glass, serve on a bed of lettuce. Serve with spring onions as a garnish.

Notes

1. Replace any hot ketchup with sriracha. Reduce siracha sauce measurements by half if your sauce is boiling.

2. Replace the wheat flour with plain flour, almond flour, or tapioca flour.)Fry chicken as required.

3. Just before serving, drizzle or coat with the sauce.

Cornflakes Chicken, Spicy (baked or fried)

Prep: 20 minutes

Cook: 15 minutes

Resting time: 30 minutes

Total Time: 35 minutes

Ingredients

- Make the marinade for the chicken.
- 1 (450 g) chicken breast, 450 g, sliced
- Two tablespoons ketchup
- Two tablespoons lemon juice

<u>Spices</u>

- One tablespoon garlic paste
- One tablespoon red pepper flakes
- 1/2 tbsp red chili powder
- 1/2 tbsp. soy sauce
- One teaspoon cumin powder
- 1/2 teaspoons of ground black pepper
- 1/4 tsp. baking powder
- 1/2 tsp salt, or to taste.
- Using flour to coat
- 1/2 cup cornstarch
- 1/3 cup all-purpose flour (or cornflour if gluten-free)
- 1/4 teaspoon salt
- 1/2 teaspoon red chili powder
- 1/2 teaspoons of oregano, if desired
- The coating of cornflakes
- two eggs.
- 1/4 teaspoon red chili powder
- 1/4 teaspoon salt
- 3 cups cornflakes, crumbled

<u>Instructions</u>

to preserve

In a bowl, mix all marinade ingredients. Refrigerate for 30 minutes or overnight.

Coat

1. Combine the flour coating ingredients in a bowl and put them aside.

2. In a separate dish, whisk together the eggs, salt, and red chili powder; set aside.

3. Maintain crumbled cornflakes in a separate dish for coating.

4. To begin with, cover all of the chicken strips with the flour mixture. Then, coat each strip with crumbled cornflakes after dipping it in the egg mixture.

For frying

Once the chicken is coated, deep fry it in small batches for 4 minutes or until golden and crispy in a pan over medium heat.

To Baking

Arrange chicken strips in a single layer on a baking pan. Spray with a bit of oil—Bake for 10 minutes at 350°F in a preheated oven.

Notes

To thaw Additionally, you may freeze coated chicken tenders. Put them on a tray and freeze. Once frozen, store in a box or freezer bag until needed. Do not defrost before frying. It will take longer to cook frozen tenders than fresh tenders.

Sesame Chicken Nugget Recipe

Prep: 20 minutes

Cook: 10 minutes

Resting time: 30 minutes

Total Time: 30 minutes

Ingredients

Marinate Chicken

- 1.500 g of boneless chicken breast, cubed

- One tablespoon lemon juice
- One tablespoon minced garlic
- 1/2 tbsp. chili powder
- 1/2 tbsp. crushed red chili
- One teaspoon chat masala
- 4 tsp. sesame seeds
- 1/2 teaspoon salt
- a single egg
- 3/4 cup cornstarch
- 1/ 4 tbsp all-purpose flour

For the final coat

- 1/2 cup cornstarch
- Two tablespoons sesame seeds
- One tablespoon chili powder
- 1/2 teaspoon salt
- Fry with oil or bake with oil spray.

Instructions

Combine the chicken and all the marinating ingredients in a mixing basin.
Combine everything and refrigerate for 30 minutes or overnight. The mixture will be thick and doughy.

Coating:

Combine cornflour, sesame seeds, red chili powder, and salt in a bowl. Coat each chicken piece entirely with the flour mixture.

Deep-fried chicken nuggets till golden brown and crunchy.

Preheat the oven to 400°F and bake the chicken nuggets for 20 minutes, or until done and golden.

Instructions for freezing:

Freeze each nugget individually on a tray. Place in a freezer bag. These chicken nuggets can keep for up to a month in the refrigerator.

No need to thaw before frying or baking. Frozen chunks will require less frying time.

Lahori Chargha Recipe fried or roasted

Prep: 10 minutes

Cook: 35 minutes

Mari nation time 4 hours

Total Time: 4 hours 45 minutes

Ingredients

- One entire chicken, about 1 kilogram-1.25 kilograms of

Marinade

- One tablespoon Kashmiri chili powder
- 1/2 tsp. cumin powder
- Two teaspoons coriander powder
- One tablespoon red pepper flakes or chili powder
- 1/2 tsp. garam masala
- 1/2 tsp. turmeric powder
- 1/2 teaspoons of ground black pepper
- 2 tsp of cornflour
- One teaspoon ginger garlic paste
- 1 tsp chat masala, plus more for sprinkling
- One teaspoon salt
- Two tablespoons oil

- Three tablespoons vinegar
- One egg
- If desired1/4 teaspoon zarda color
- Oil for frying
- Two tablespoons lemon juice

sides:

- Salad leaves
- green chutney
- Slices of onion
- Garlic raita
- French fries
- A spicy ketchup

Instructions

Prepared Chicken

With a kitchen towel, wash and pat dry. Make profound letter V-shaped slashes in the chicken breast with a sharp knife. Similarly, make 1-2 deep incisions along the length of the leg parts. Place aside.

Marinate

Combine all ingredients under "charge marinade" in a bowl. This marinade is sufficient for one to one and a half kg of chicken.

Take a tablespoon of the marinade in your palm and spread it evenly over the chicken. Avoid spice burns by wearing gloves. Additionally, secure the chicken's legs with a cotton thread.

Marinate the chicken for 4 hours on the counter or overnight in the fridge. After that, add the chicken to the steamer. Assure that the water level in the steamer is at least 12 inches below the steaming plate. 25 minutes steamed until chicken is tender. The chicken should be removed from the steamer and placed aside.

Fry charge

Before frying the chicken, prepare the tray with fried or baked potatoes, fresh vegetables, green chutney, and garlic dip.

2-3 inches of oil in a nonstick wok On a medium burner, heat the oil and add the steamed charge. Cook, occasionally stirring, until the chicken is well cooked and browned. With two tongs, turn and remove the chicken. Serve the crispy fried chicken on a dish.

Notes

Charge, baking, or roasting in the oven:

The roast charge for 1 hour or longer at 350°F or 180°C on a baking sheet covered with butter paper. A meat thermometer should read 165°F for safety. Cooking time is based on a 1 kg whole chicken; larger birds will take longer.

Charge Rotisserie

Roast for 25-30 minutes at 350 degrees Fahrenheit or until the internal temperature reaches 165 degrees Fahrenheit. Timings are based on a 1 kg whole chicken; cooking time would increase for a giant bird.

Instructions for reheating

The charge can be reheated in a steamer for moist heat.

Preparation instructions

1. The charge can be steamed for a few hours before frying. Before frying, ensure that the account is at room temperature or slightly heated.
2. An excess charge may be used in place of leftover rotisserie chicken in most recipes.

Chicken Tikka Karahi, Balochi style

Prep: 20 minutes

Cook: 25 minutes

Total Time: 45 minutes

Ingredients

- Balochi Karahi Masala or Spice Mix

Whole Spices

- 3/4 tbsp Coriander seeds
- 1/2 tbsp. crushed red pepper
- 1/2 tbsp. cumin seeds
- 1 tsp freshly ground black pepper
- Spices, powdered
- Add 1/2 tbsp of Kashmiri chili powder or tandoori masala
- 1/2 tbsp fenugreek leaves, dried
- 1/2 teaspoon chat masala
- 1/2 teaspoon garam masala
- 1/2 teaspoon turmeric
- 1/2 teaspoon black or pink salt

Balochi Chicken Tikka Karahi

- 750 g of skinless chicken breast chunks (1 medium chicken cut into eight pieces)
- 1 cup of water
- One teaspoon salt
- Oil for frying
- Five fat garlic cloves, roughly chopped into approximately three tablespoons

- 1 inch coarsely chopped ginger (about two tablespoons)
- 6-8 slitted green chilies
- Two tablespoons of coriander
- 3–4 tablespoons lemon juice

Instructions

Balochi Karahi masala

1. After a minute, take whole spices from the stove and whisk in powdered spices. Now, finely grind the spices.
2. The Baluchi Karahi masala has been prepared. Refrigerate the spice mixture in an airtight container.

Balochi Tikka Karahi

1. Soak chicken for 20 minutes in water and salt. (Complete this step before preparing the spice blend to save time.)
2. Now, in a karahi or wok, combine the soaked chicken and brine water and add enough oil to nearly fully cover the chicken.
3. Over high heat, I am often stirring.
4. Add the ginger and garlic after 15 minutes on high heat. Continue cooking.
5. When the majority of the water has evaporated, and the oil has ceased to bubble, add the green chilies as well.
6. After around 20–25 minutes, the chicken should begin to turn golden. Continue stirring at rapid intervals to brown the chicken until lightly browned evenly. Avoid over-frying.
7. 7. Set a metal colander over the skillet. Separate the oil and spices from the chicken by straining. Reintroduce fried chicken to the wok or karahi.

8. 3-4 teaspoons of prepared Balochi spice mix, fresh coriander, and lemon juice. Combine well and cover the wok. Allow 7 minutes for the chicken to absorb the flavor. Following that, serve!

-

Bohra Fried Chicken, soft and succulent

Prep: 20 minutes

Cook: 30 minutes

Resting time: 30 minutes

Total Time: 50 minutes

Servings: servings (12 pieces)

Ingredients

Marinate Chicken

- 750 g skinless, bone-in chicken (thighs and drumsticks preferred)
- One medium pureed tomato
- Five tablespoons lemon juice or three tablespoons vinegar
- 2 tbsp. yogurt
- 2 tbsp olive oil
- 1–2 tbsp. minced green chili, serrano, or other hot pepper
- One tablespoon grated ginger
- One tablespoon minced garlic
- One tablespoon cumin powder
- One tablespoon coriander powder
- 1/2 tbsp. Kashmiri chili powder or paprika
- 3/4 tsp salt
- 1/2 tsp. turmeric
- 1/2 teaspoon of ground black pepper

Coating:

- 1/2 cups bread crumbs, plus additional for coating
- Two large eggs, separated yolk, and white
- a pinch of salt
- 1/4 teaspoon red chili powder
- Two tablespoons water
- Oil for deep frying

Instructions

Chicken Marinate

1. In a saucepan, mix together all marinade ingredients for 30 minutes.
2. Prepare chicken
3. Cook marinated chicken for 20 minutes over medium heat or thoroughly cooked and tender (but not falling off the bones).
4. Then, with continuous stirring, cook the extra water over high heat until a vibrant sauce coats the chicken. Turn off the heat and chill.

Chicken Coat

Now, add breadcrumbs to the saucepan and shake it vigorously with the handles to combine everything. Coat the chicken with moist crumbs from the saucepan, squeezing the poultry lightly in the fist to coat it firmly. (Wear gloves when handling food to prevent chili burns.)

Make an egg wash

1. In a bowl, whisk egg whites for a minute with a hand whisk until frothy.
2. Then whisk together the egg yolks, red chili powder, salt, and water. Now combine the egg yolks and whites.

Make some chicken fries.

In a saucepan, heat about 2 inches of oil. Dip each piece of chicken in the egg wash and then deep-fry until golden brown. Serve immediately with a dip or chutney of your choice.

Notes

The recipe has been tested both with and without tomatoes. Tomatoes help maintain the bread crumb coating fresh and tasty, which is why I recommend adding a pureed tomato in the background. You may also use one tablespoon of tomato paste or ketchup in place of the tomato.

I used extremely hot and thin green chilies. Because the bread crumb coating absorbs the masala and dilutes the flavors, begin with a robustly flavored sauce.

Keema Naan

Prep: 2 hours

Cook: 30 minutes

Total Time: 2 hours 30 minutes

Servings : servings (4 Naan)

Ingredients

For the dough

- 4 cup (500 g) plain flour + extra for dusting
- Four tablespoons yogurt
- Two teaspoon salt
- 1/2 teaspoon sugar
- Two teaspoons active dry yeast
- 2 tbsp oil
- 1/2 cups milk

- 1/2 cups of lukewarm water or more as necessary.

For the stuffing

- 500-gram ground meat (lamb, beef, or chicken), finely processed once more in a food processor
- 1 cup finely chopped onions (approximately 1.5 cups)
- Two tablespoons ginger paste
- One tablespoon minced garlic
- One tablespoon dried pomegranate arils, one tablespoon pomegranate molasses, or two tablespoons of lemon juice
- 1 tbsp crushed coriander seeds, preferably roasted
- 1 tbsp toasted and crushed cumin seeds
- red chili flakes (1/2 tbsp)
- One teaspoon salt
- 1/2 teaspoon red chili powder (omit if you prefer a milder flavor).
- 1/2 tsp. turmeric
- 1/2 tsp freshly ground black pepper
- 2 tbsp. of butter
- Three tablespoons finely chopped green chili
- 1/2 cups of coriander, cilantro, or coriander leaves
- 1/4 cup chopped mint leaves

For Naan

- 1/2 cup plain yogurt
- Two tablespoons sesame seeds
- Two tablespoons butter or olive oil for brushing

<u>Instructions</u>

The preparation of the dough

Combine flour, yogurt, eggs, salt, sugar, and yeast in a mixing dish. The consistency of the mixture will be crumbly.

1. To activate the yeast, combine it with sugar and warm water in a basin and allow it to rise for 5 minutes. This step is unnecessary if using quick yeast from a packet.

2. Gradually add milk and use your hands to blend the flour. Then, as required, add water until a soft dough forms.

3. Drizzle a small amount of oil over the dough and evenly coat. Cover the bowl and store it in an excellent, dry location. 1 hour to double the dough

Marinated the stuffing

1. Prepare the stuffing while the dough rises. Set aside the stuffing ingredients in a bowl.

The mince should be finely ground, which may be accomplished by pounding the mince in the chopper once more. If you desire to use prepared mince filling, see the notes section.

For Naan

1. Punch the air out of the dough when it has doubled in size. Then move the dough with a spatula. Grease your palm with oil and knead for a minute.

2. Separate the dough into four equal halves. Flour each dough ball and roll it into a 4-inch round.

3. Stuff the center with filling and pull the ends together by squeezing all the corners to form a filled dough ball.

4. Prep the oven top grill to 400 degrees Fahrenheit or 200 degrees Celsius.

5. Dust with flour and gently roll into naan. Create depressions all around you with your fingertips to slightly higher corners than the center.

6. Poke holes all over the dough with the bottom of a wooden spoon to prevent the naan from bubbling while cooking.

Cook Naan

1. A grill (Tawa) or nonstick pan should be preheated. Transfer the naan to the pan using a plate. (To raise the naan, slide a flat plate beneath it.) Brush yogurt on the top and sides of the naan and sprinkle with sesame seeds. Cook for 5-7 minutes on low heat or until golden brown.

2. Then transfer the naan to the oven's center rack. Additionally, the broiler should be lit concurrently with the stove. Bake for 5-7 minutes, or until the top of the naan is golden brown. Naan should be transferred to a platter and brushed with melted butter or oil. Serve it immediately after baking.

Notes

How to prepare cooked keema stuffing: Combine the minced beef and 12 cups of water in a saucepan. Cook until the water evaporates. Fry the mince in the oil now. combine all the spices, except the green chilies, 12 chopped onions, and coriander. Allow the mince to cook until it is brown and cooked through. Combine the onion, green chilies, coriander, and mint leaves with the hot keema and remove it from the heat. Allow it to cool. Keema filling must be completely dry. (If cooking naan on the stovetop without an oven, use cooked keema filling.)

Cooking instructions without using an oven: Following the "For Naan" steps for these stages, Wet the bottom surface of the naan with a small amount of water. Then transfer the wet naan to a Tawa or pan with handles. Then, cook the naan on medium heat for 6–8 minutes. The naan should adhere to the Tawa or pan due to the moist bottom. (Avoid using a nonstick pan.) Turn the tawa or pan over to expose the naan's top surface to direct heat. This will roast the top surface, giving it oven-like marks and crispiness. Adjust the naan's distance from the flame as necessary and cook evenly until golden markings appear.

Store cooked naan:

Cooked naan should be stored in the following manner: Cover the naan with a towel to keep it. Allow the naan to cool completely before storing it at room temperature for a few hours or in the refrigerator for 2-3 days. Similarly, you can freeze naan. Defrost thoroughly before reheating.

To reheat:

spritz the naan with water. Brush a minimal amount of oil all over and then reheat for 5 minutes on the wire rack in the oven. Cover with a lid for 2 minutes to reheat naan on a Tawa, then turn and warm thoroughly.

Chicken Penne Pasta Recipe with white sauce

Prep: 15 minutes

Cook: 40 minutes

Total Time: 55 minutes

Equipment

casserole

Ingredients

Make Chicken

- Two tablespoons oil
- 1 tbsp ginger garlic paste

- One tablespoon chili paste
- chicken (400 g)
- 1/4 teaspoon salt (to taste)

Produce white sauce.

- 1 quart of oil
- a quarter cup of flour
- One nos cubed chicken
- 1 tsp freshly ground black pepper
- 1/2 teaspoon oregano
- 4 cup milk

Other

- 1.5 cups uncooked penne noodles (boiled according to package directions with salt)
- 1 Tin (drained) corn
- One chopped green onion stalk
- 1-2 green chilies, chopped
- One teaspoon dried basil
- 1/2 tsp. salt (or to taste)
- 75 gram of cheese, plus some extra for garnish.
- Garnish
- 1/4 teaspoons of oregano, dry

Instructions

1. Using a saucepan, mix together everything you'll need for the chicken. Let it simmer until the chicken is cooked and the juices have disappeared. Place aside.

2. In a separate saucepan, heat the oil and sauté the flour, chicken cubes, oregano, and black pepper for 1 minute over low heat.

3. Then, gradually add milk to the flour while continually stirring. If there are any flour lumps, break them up. Stir in the white sauce until smooth and bubbly.

4. Remove from the heat and whisk in the remaining ingredients listed in the Others section.

5. Transfer the chicken pasta to a 1.5-liter oven-safe dish and top with additional cheese.

6. Just before serving, bake at 350°F for 10 minutes, or until bubbly. Then broil for 2-4 minutes until browned. Serve it right away.

Notes

Make it fresh and serve it promptly for the most delicate flavor. On the other hand, this dish may be prepared up to 24 hours ahead and refrigerated. Just before serving, bake. Leftovers may also be warmed in a skillet over low heat with a splash of milk.

Spinach Chicken Lasagne Recipe

Prep: 30 minutes

Cook: 30 minutes

Total Time: 1 hour

Ingredients

For Spinach Chicken Filling

- One tablespoon oil
- 1 tbsp. minced garlic
- 500 grams chicken breast or 1.5 cups cooked shredded chicken

- 1/2 tsp freshly ground black pepper
- Optional: 1/2-1 tablespoon chopped green chili
- 1 tsp dried oregano
- 1 cup boiling spinach, one can mushroom
- Three pureed tomatoes or three tablespoons tomato paste.
- 3 tbsp hot tomato ketchup or chili garlic sauce

Vegetables with white sauce

- Four tablespoons butter
- Five tablespoons flour
- One chicken cube/bullion
- 2 cups milk
- Two green onions, sliced
- Two tablespoons coriander or parsley
- One sliced green chili, optional

Assembling

- Five lasagna sheets, cooked as directed on the package
- 1 cup cheddar cheese (or other melted cheese)
- 1 cup mozzarella cheese, shredded

Instructions

Filling: Chicken Spinach

1. In a skillet, heat the oil and softly sauté the garlic. Add the cubed chicken, chopped chilies (optional), oregano, cumin, pepper, and salt. Then boil for 2-3 minutes over medium heat until the chicken is white.

2. At this point, add the tomato sauce, tomato puree, and spinach. Continue to cook after thoroughly combining all of the ingredients.

3. Cook, covered until the chicken is cooked through and the liquid has evaporated. Set apart from the heat.

Vegetables with white sauce

1. Melt the butter in a small pot. Combine the flour and chicken cubes. Fry until the flour begins to smell aromatic.

2. Add the milk gradually while stirring constantly. Break apart any lumps.

3. Heat the sauce until it bubbles. After that, add the vegetables. The sauce is ready after thorough mixing.

Lasagna Layering

1. Begin by coating the bottom of an 8 x 8-inch square casserole or baking dish with a thin layer of white sauce.

2. Stack lasagna sheets on top.

3. Then spread half of the spinach chicken filling on top.

4. Spread half of the white sauce on top. We have just completed the first set of layers.

5. Use leftover spinach chicken stuffing and white sauce to make lasagna

6. a thick covering of cheese

Savory Chicken Crepe Recipe

Prep: 20 minutes

Cook: 30 minutes

Total Time: 50 minutes

Servings: rolls

Ingredients

Make Crepes

- 1 1/2 cups milk

- 1 cup of flour
- four eggs
- Three tablespoons butter
- 1/4 teaspoon salt
- Oil for pan lubrication

Prepare Chicken

- 400 g skinless, boneless chicken
- 1/2 tsp. ginger paste
- 1/2 tsp. garlic paste
- One tablespoon chili paste
- 1/2 cups water
- 1 tbsp. oil

Prepare a white sauce.

- Six tablespoons oil
- 1 tbsp. minced garlic
- Seven tablespoons plain flour
- One chicken or bouillon cube
- a quarter teaspoon dried oregano
- 1/4 teaspoon black pepper, ground
- milk (3 1/2 c.)

vegetable

- One large stalk of finely chopped green onions
- One medium chopped capsicum
- 3-5 finely chopped medium green chilies. Adjust the chilies to taste, or leave them out entirely.)
- 100 g cheddar cheese, to be used as a garnish

- If desired, 1/4 teaspoon dried oregano

Instructions

Prepare Crepes

1. To begin, fill a blender halfway with milk. After that, whisk in the eggs, flour, butter, and salt. For a minute, blend until a smooth purée form.

2. Place the batter in the refrigerator for 30 minutes to chill.

3. Heat a nonstick skillet over medium heat and coat with a few drops of oil. Then pour 1/3 cup of batter into the prepared pan and cook for a few minutes, or until the edges begin to dry and become slightly yellow. Then turn the crepe over and cook for a few seconds on the other side, or until it has a few brown spots. Take the crepe out of the pan and set it aside.

4. Continue with the remaining batter to create approximately ten crepes. Crepes should be piled one on top of the other and laid aside.

Prepare Chicken

1. While the batter chills in the refrigerator, prepare the chicken. Combine the chicken, ginger, garlic, green paste, saltwater, and oil in a pan. Combing well and covering. 20 minutes till soft.

2. Dry off any excess water on a hot day.

Produce white sauce.

1. Heat the oil in a small skillet and sauté the garlic.

2. Stir in flour, pepper, cubes of chicken, and oregano. 3. On medium heat, combine and simmer for 2 minutes or until aromatic.

3. Lower the heat to a low simmer and gradually whisk in the milk, stirring constantly. Cook for several minutes, or until the liquid comes to a boil and turns thick. (If necessary, adjust the flame.)

4. Stir in the remaining vegetables and chicken to the white sauce. Combine thoroughly.

To assemble:

1. Arrange crepes on a platter and fill with about 1/2 cup filling. Fold the crepe's top and bottom edges over the filling. Then, fold the right and left sides together to form a crepe roll. Assemble the remaining crepes similarly.

2. Place each bun in an ovenproof plate and top with cheese.

3. Bake for 7 minutes at 350°F/160°C in a preheated oven. Then broil for 5 minutes, or until the dish is slightly brown.

4. Serve with tomato sauce and garnished with dried oregano.

Tikka Paratha roll bake recipe

Prep: 30 minutes

Cook: 20 minutes

Total Time: 50 minutes

Ingredients

Chicken Marinade

- One boneless chicken breast, sliced
- 3 tbsp Chicken Tikka Spice Mix
- Two tablespoons cream
- 2 tbsp. yogurt (Dahi)
- Two tablespoons ginger garlic paste
- 1/2 teaspoons of ground black pepper (kali Mirch)
- a quarter cup of oil (tel)

Roll paratha ingredients.

- 1 cup mayonnaise

- 1/2 cup of tamarind chutney (imli)
- 1/2 cups of chutney with coriander and mint (dhania pudina)
- Three chopped jalapeno peppers (Garmiani Hari Mirch)
- One tablespoon minced garlic
- One large onion, peeled
- Two chopped capsicum (Shimla Mirch)
- Five frozen parathas
- 1cup milk

Garnish

- 2 tbsp. sliced olives
- 1/2 cups of Swiss cheese
- 1/2 chopped capsicum

Instructions

1. In a mixing dish, combine all of the chicken marinade ingredients. Additionally, set aside 30 minutes.
2. In a saucepan over medium-low heat, cook marinated chicken until thoroughly cooked. (Approximately 20 minutes).
3. In a mixing bowl, combine mayonnaise, mint, coriander chutney, garlic, and chopped chilies. Combine the onions and capsicum well and leave aside.
4. Grease a 5" x 8" baking dish and preheat the oven to 350 F.
5. Keep a milk dish handy—Fry frozen paratha without using oil in a nonstick skillet. Dip the heated paratha in milk for 5 seconds and immediately put it on the greased baking tray. Rep with the remaining four parathas.

6. Divide cooked chicken tikka into six equal portions. Each paratha should be stuffed with the chicken and chutney mixture and then rolled. Similarly, fill and move all the parathas. Reserving the sixth portion of chicken for garnish

7. Arrange the leftover chicken, capsicum rings, olives, and chutney mixture on top of the rolls. Ascertain that the food is juicy.

8. Top with shredded cheddar cheese. Bake for 10 minutes, or until the dish is well cooked, and the cheese has melted. It's time to serve the chicken tikka paratha roll bake.

Bread Lasagna with chicken and veggies

Prep: 20 minutes

Cook: 30 minutes

Total Time: 50 minutes

Ingredients

Chicken

- 1.400 g skinless, boneless chicken breast
- 1 tbsp green chili paste
- One tablespoon garlic ginger paste
- Two tablespoons olive oil
- salt and pepper to taste.

Crust bread

- Four medium bread slices, or enough to cover the entire base
- 3/4 cup milk
- Five tablespoons mayonnaise
- Two tablespoons tomato ketchup

- One tablespoon chili-garlic sauce

- One teaspoon mustard sauce

- One teaspoon hot sauce

- One teaspoon soy sauce

Vegetables with white sauce

- 4 tbsp. of oil or butter

- 5 tsp unbleached flour

- 1/2 cubes of chicken (or 1 tbsp chicken powder)

- 1/2 tsp of pepper

- 1/2 teaspoons of dried oregano

- 1/2 tsp. salt (or to taste)

- 2 cups of lukewarm milk

- If desired, two jalapeno peppers

- 2 to 3 tablespoons of fresh coriander, chopped, optional

- 1 cup chopped mixed vegetables (capsicum, green onions, carrots, broccoli, etc.)

- 1 cup fresh steamed corn or canned corn

- 1/2 cup shredded cheddar cheese

Instructions

1. oven to 350 degrees F.

2. Toss the chicken with ginger-garlic paste, green chili paste, salt, and oil. Cook until the chicken is tender and the liquid has evaporated.

3. Trim the edges of the loaves and soak them briefly in milk before placing them on a plate.

4. In a bowl, whisk together mayonnaise, chili garlic sauce, tomato ketchup, mustard, chile, and soy sauce. Distribute the sauce mixture over the bread layer.

5. Arrange a layer of boneless chicken on top of the sauce.

6. To prepare the white sauce, heat oil in a saucepan over low heat and whisk flour. Fry for a further 10 seconds before adding the salt, pepper, oregano, and chicken cube. Switch off the heat and add the heated milk. I am combing well to get a smooth sauce. Bring the white sauce back to a boil. Switch off the heat.

7. Mix the corn, jalapeño, and veggies with the spicy white sauce. Combine all ingredients and pour the sauce over the chicken in the dish.

8. Arrange cheese, olives, and mushrooms on top of the white sauce.

9. Bake for 10-15 minutes, or until the cheese has melted and the dish is steaming hot.

Lagan Ki Seekh

Prep: 20 minutes

Cook: 30 minutes

Total Time: 3 hours

Ingredients

Marination

- 500 g minced beef (beef, mutton, or lamb keema)
- 1 1/2 tbsp ginger paste
- 1/2 tbsp garlic paste (lahsun)
- 1 tbsp chili paste (Hari Mirch)
- 1 tbsp freshly chopped coriander (hara dhania)
- One tablespoon minced mint (pudina)

- 2 tsp. chili powder (Lal Mirch)
- 1/2 tsp coriander powder (dhania)
- 1/2 tsp. turmeric powder (Haldi)
- One teaspoon Garam Masala (garam masala) powder
- 1/2 tsp cumin powder
- salt and pepper to taste.

Assembling

- 150 grams or one large onion, cooked until golden (all piyaz)
- Six tablespoons oil (tel)
- Four slices of medium-sized bread
- 1/4 cup milk, or more
- Four eggs (every day)
- 2 tbsp lemon juice
- Decorate with julienned ginger and chopped coriander
- For serving, add ketchup and lemon.

Instructions

Marination

1. Clean the mince by rinsing and straining it. Excess water can be removed by pressing mince with a big spoon strainer.

2. Combine minced meat, ginger, garlic, green chili, mint, and fresh coriander in a bowl along with 1/2 teaspoon each of red chili, coriander, turmeric, salt, cumin, and allspice powder. Combine them and marinate for 2 hours. At this point, you may smoke qeema.

Baking and Assembling

1. Preheat the oven to 350°F and grease an 8" x 5" baking dish.

2. Bread and milk in a small bowl. Combine thoroughly to get a lump-free mixture. If necessary, add additional milk. Place aside.

3. Set aside the crushed fried onion.

4. Then add the fried onions and toast.

5. Mix in 1 beaten egg and lemon juice.

6. Evenly distribute the mince mixture in an 8" x 5 "baking dish; the mixture layer should be 1.5 inches thick.

7. Lightly beat three eggs with 12 red chili powder and salt teaspoons. Over the minced meat, pour a layer of eggs.

8. Bring the oil to a boil and then pour it evenly over the eggs. (You may use the same oil used to sauté the onions.)

9. Place the dish in the oven and bake for 30 to 35 minutes on the lowest shelf at gas mark 6, 200 C, or 400 F. After 15 minutes, rotate the tray to ensure equal cooking. When the eggs are boiled, lagan ki seekh is ready.

Lagan ki seekh (gluten free)

Prep: 15 minutes

Cook: 30 minutes

Total Time: 45 minutes

Ingredients

- 500 g mutton or beef mince
- cooking oil
- One large fried onion (approximately 1/2 cup fried onions)
- Three peeled and chunked potatoes

List 1

- One teaspoon green chili paste

- Two tablespoons ginger garlic paste
- 1/2–1 tsp red chili powder
- One teaspoon turmeric powder
- 1 tsp toasted cumin seeds
- One teaspoon of toasted coriander seeds
- 1/2 teaspoon salt (more for eggs):
- One tablespoon clarified butter
- 3 tsp. chopped coriander

Other

- Five sliced eggs
- ketchup or garlic chili sauce

Instructions

1. oven to 180 °C/gas mark 4
2. Fry the potatoes in a wok till golden. Drain any excess oil before mashing the potatoes and setting them aside.
3. Grind or smash the onions in the same oil. Dispose of. Combine mince, mashed potatoes, onion, one egg, and the rest of the ingredients. a good combination
4. Lightly oil a platter and evenly distribute the meat mince.
5. Beat the remaining four eggs with salt and 1/4 teaspoon red chili powder—eggs over the mincemeat.
6. Pour 1/4 cup of hot oil (from onions and potatoes) over the eggs.
7. Bake for 25–30 minutes, or until the eggs are cooked through.
8. Cut into six, with ketchup or chili garlic sauce.

Notes

1. Make use of pre-fried onions.

2. Instead of frying potatoes, boil them.

3. Roasted cumin and coriander in a bottle. To save time, use ground cumin and coriander.

Dabba Chicken Pie

Prep: 15 minutes

Cook: 30 minutes

Total Time: 45 minutes

Ingredients

- 1 cup elbow (macaroni) pasta
- Three tablespoons oil
- One tablespoon minced garlic
- One tablespoon grated ginger
- 1-11/2 Tbsp. chopped green chili
- One teaspoon cumin powder
- 1/2–1 teaspoon ground black pepper
- Substitute almond powder or plain flour for 2 tbsp of cashew powder.
- 1/2 cup of whipped yogurt
- 500 g of boneless chicken
- 1 cup coconut milk
- 1/2 cup boiled corn
- 1/2 cup carrots, diced
- 1/4 cup capsicum
- Two tablespoons fresh coriander
- 1/2 cup heavy cream

Other

- three whipped eggs
- 1/4 teaspoon chili powder
- 1/4 teaspoon salt
- Tomato garnished with slices
- Capsicum, thinly sliced
- Drizzled with 3 tbsp oil

Instructions

1. Cook elbow pasta for 1 minute less than directed on the package. Rinse pasta in cold water after draining boiling water. Drizzle a thin layer of oil over the spaghetti. Dispose of.

2. Then add the chicken and toss for a few seconds. Cover and thoroughly combine 15 minutes on low heat until tender.

3. Stir in the cooked spaghetti corn, carrots, and capsicum. Cover and thoroughly combine. Cook for 5-7 minutes more, until soft. Reduce the heat.

4. Now add cream and fresh coriander. Simmer for 1-2 minutes. Then remove from the heat.

5. Sliced tomatoes and capsicum garnish

6. Whisk together three eggs, salt, and red chili powder. Over the spaghetti, whipped eggs.

7. Finally, heat the oil in the vessel until it smokes. Drizzle oil over the eggs.

8. Cook the pie, covered, on low heat for 5-7 minutes, or until it is set.

9. Cut into slices and serve immediately.

Bohra Red Chicken

Prep: 10 minutes

Cook: 20 minutes

Total Time: 30 minutes

Ingredients

Marination

- 1-kilogram skinless whole chicken or eight pieces of chicken
- 5 tbsp Chicken Tikka Spice Mix
- Two tablespoons ginger garlic paste
- Four tablespoons yogurt
- Two tablespoons butter
- Two tablespoons lemon juice

Sauce

- a half-cup tomato ketchup
- 1/4 cup garlic sauce
- 1 cup heavy cream
- 1 cup steamed vegetables (carrots, capsicums, and potatoes)

Tempering

- Two tablespoons oil
- 1/4 teaspoon cumin
- 1/4 tsp. mustard seeds
- 5-6 button red chilies, sliced

Smoke

- a piece of charcoal about 2 inches long
- a few drops of essential oil
- One hard-boiled egg for garnish
- a sprinkling of fresh coriander
- One packets Slims chips (potato sticks)
- Three to four salad leaves

Instructions

Marination

1. Wash and dry the chicken with a napkin. Make deep incisions and stab the chicken with a fork.

2. Combine all of the marinade ingredients and thoroughly coat the chicken.

3. Refrigerate overnight to marinate.

Cooking

1. Cook the chicken for 20 minutes, or until done the next day. On a high flame, burn all the water. Sear (bhuna) the chicken on a hot flame for a few minutes. Your chicken is now prepared.

2. In a mixing bowl, combine all sauce ingredients and set aside. Before serving, thoroughly cook the chicken and pour the sauce over it. Cook for a few minutes, covered. Avoid overcooking.

3. Steam the vegetables and combine them with the chicken. At this point, you can also smoke the chicken with a piece of red-hot coal and a few drops of oil.

4. In a saucepan, heat the oil and add the cumin, mustard, and red chili. Allow the red chilies to darken slightly before pouring the tempering over the chicken.

5. Garnish with desired garnishes.

Cheesy Spaghetti Balls Recipe

Prep: 20 minutes

Cook: 30 minutes

Total Time: 50 minutes

Servings: balls

Ingredients

For Chicken

- 300 g of boneless, skinless chicken
- One tablespoon green chili paste
- 1 tbsp ginger garlic paste
- 1/2 cup water

white sauce

- Four tablespoons butter
- Four tablespoons flour
- 1 tbsp chicken powder
- 1/2 tsp freshly ground black pepper
- 1/2 teaspoons of dried oregano
- 1 cup milk
- Three cheese triangles or 1/2 cup shredded cheddar cheese
- 1 cup shattered spaghetti
- Boil a pot of water.
- Salt and pepper to taste.

Vegetables

- One large shredded carrot
- One large finely chopped green onion stalk
- One capsicum, finely chopped
- 2 tbsp. chopped coriander leaves, optional
- 2 tbsp. chopped green chilies
- One tablespoon red chili sauce

Coating

- 1/2 cup all-purpose flour
- There are two eggs.

- 1/2 tsp. salt
- 1/2 tsp. red chili powder
- 1 1/2 tbsp. bread crumbs
- Oil for frying

Instructions

Boiling Chickens

1. In a pot, combine boneless chicken, green chili paste, ginger garlic paste, and water. Cook for 20 minutes over medium heat or until the chicken is cooked. On high heat, evaporate any residual water in the pot.

2. Bring the chicken to room temperature before shredding. Place aside.

Regarding white sauce

1. melt butter over low heat in a heavy-bottomed saucepan or pot. Combine flour, black pepper, oregano powder, and chicken cubes or powder in a medium mixing bowl. After a few minutes, gradually add 1 cup of milk while stirring constantly. This white sauce will be more viscous in consistency than conventional white sauce. Place aside.

Water Spaghetti

While preparing the white sauce, bring a saucepan of salted water to a boil. Cook spaghetti according to the package directions until al dente or cooked through.

Assemble the spaghetti sauce.

3. Drain excess water from the pasta and add it to the white sauce. Additionally, shredded chicken and cheese should be added. Combine thoroughly. (Refrigerate the mixture while chopping the vegetables.)

4. Once the white sauce mixture has reached room temperature, stir in the chopped veggies and red chili sauce. (Refrigerate until the cooled mixture is easy to roll.)

Bread crumb coating on both sides:

1. Whisk together two eggs, salt, one tablespoon of water, and red chili powder in a mixing bowl. Place aside.

2. Flour a plate and set it aside. Pour the flour over the tightly packed spaghetti mixture in a 14-cup measuring cup. Form 12 balls by rolling them in flour.

3. Dip each ball in egg, then in bread crumbs. Roll once more in the egg mixture and bread crumbs to coat twice with bread crumbs.

To deep fry

1. Heat the oil in a wok over medium-high heat and deep fry until brown, stirring 3–4 times.

2. Alternatively, store in the refrigerator for up to 24 hours before frying.

3. Garnish with spicy tomato ketchup and lemon wedges and serve immediately.

<u>Notes</u>

To determine the quantity of spaghetti: Break several small bunches of spaghetti into 1-inch pieces and place them in a cup to create a full cup of broken spaghetti.

Maggie Noodle Omelet

Prep: 10 minutes

Cook: 10 minutes

Total Time: 20 minutes

Ingredients

Filling

- 1/2 tablespoon mayonnaise
- Two tablespoons chili garlic sauce
- Two tablespoons corn
- Three tablespoons grated carrot
- Two tablespoons finely chopped capsicum
- One tablespoon finely chopped green onion
- 1 tbsp. chopped coriander
- One teaspoon freshly minced garlic
- darmiyan hari mirch,1 1/2 teaspoons green chilies
- 1/8 tsp. pepper

Topping

- a third of a cup (60 g) shredded cheddar

A combination of egg noodles

- a single quick noodle (in a spicy flavor similar to masala noodles)
- 1/2 cup of water
- Four large eggs
- 1/4 cubes of chicken
- One tablespoon lemon juice
- 1/2 teaspoon red chili powder
- salt and pepper to taste.
- Two tablespoons oil

Instructions

1. Bring 1/2 cup of water and half a packet of flavor enhancers to a boil with the noodles. Cool.

2. In a bowl, combine mayonnaise, chili, garlic sauce, pepper, and vegetables. Place aside.

3. In a separate bowl, crack eggs. Combine the remaining half-package of flavor enhancer, lemon juice, red chili powder, and chicken cube in the egg. Whisk vigorously. Now, add the instant noodles and gently combine.

4. In a nonstick frying pan over medium-high heat, heat the oil. Spread half of the egg noodle mixture in an omelet fashion. Reduce to a medium heat setting.

5. Spread the second layer of vegetable filling on the egg noodle mixture. Shredded cheese should be evenly distributed over the veggie filling.

6. Pour in the remainder of the egg-noodle mixture. (Make the layers rapidly to avoid overcooking the egg base.)

7. Transfer the omelet to a serving platter. A hot frying pan should be used to cover the plate. Additionally, flip gently. Cook for 1-2 minutes more or until done. To serve, slice into triangles.

8. Serve with ketchup.

Notes: If the omelet spreads or breaks while flipping, use a spatula to put it back together in a circle. It will take on an excellent shape as it cooks.

Made in the USA
Las Vegas, NV
26 February 2022

44634863R00044